© 2024 by FAISAL JAMIL. All rights reserved.

Title: "Mastering Territory Management: Strategies for Success"

This book, along with its contents encompassing text, illustrations, images, diagrams, and other creative elements, is the exclusive property of FAISAL JAMIL and is safeguarded by copyright law.

FAISAL JAMIL asserts full ownership and retains all rights to this book. No part of this publication may be reproduced, distributed, or transmitted in any form or by any means, such as photocopying, recording, or electronic methods, without prior written consent from the copyright holder. Brief quotations in critical reviews and certain noncommercial uses permitted by copyright law are exceptions.

This copyright notice applies to all editions, formats, and translations of the book, whether in print, digital, or any other medium or technology existing now or developed in the future. Unauthorized use or infringement may result in legal action and pursuit of remedies under applicable copyright laws.

While efforts have been made to ensure accuracy and reliability, FAISAL JAMIL does not guarantee the completeness or suitability of the information. Readers are responsible for evaluating and using the content judiciously.

FAISAL JAMIL reserves the right to make changes, updates, or corrections to the book without prior notice. Inclusion of third-party materials or references does not imply endorsement or affiliation unless used under fair use principles or with proper permissions and attributions.

For permissions, inquiries, or requests regarding the book's use, please contact FAISAL JAMIL through official channels listed on their Amazon author page or provided email address.

This comprehensive copyright notice serves to protect FAISAL JAMIL'S intellectual property rights, maintain content control, and inform users about associated restrictions and permissions.

Warm regards,

FAISAL JAMIL

For your feedback and reviews:

http://www.amazon.com/author/faisal.jamil

Email: faisaljamilauthor@gmail.com

About the author

Certainly! Faisal Jamil is a multifaceted individual with a diverse set of skills and experiences. With a strong foundation in computer knowledge since childhood, he has developed a deep understanding of technology that informs his work as a content writer. Faisal also possesses digital skills, which further enhance his abilities in various digital platforms and technologies.

Beyond his professional endeavors, Faisal Jamil has also excelled in the martial arts, particularly Shotokan Karate, where he achieved the prestigious rank of first Dan black belt. This achievement speaks to his dedication, discipline, and commitment to personal growth and mastery.

In his professional life, Faisal Jamil has carved out a successful career in sales management within the Fast Moving Consumer Goods (FMCG) sector. His roles in various FMCG companies have honed his skills in strategic planning, team leadership, and business development. Faisal's ability to drive sales and achieve targets has been instrumental in his career progression, showcasing his talent for identifying opportunities and delivering results.

Faisal Jamil is also deeply interested in business investment strategies, planning, and execution. His understanding of these areas has been key to his success in the business world, allowing him to make informed decisions and implement effective strategies. His ability to navigate the complexities of investment planning and execution has set him apart as a strategic thinker and a valuable asset in any business endeavor.

Overall, Faisal Jamil is a dynamic individual who combines his passion for technology, martial arts, sales management, digital skills, and business investment strategies to achieve success in diverse fields. His journey is a testament to his versatility, resilience, and continuous pursuit of excellence.

Yours Sincerely

FAISAL JAMIL

For your feedback and reviews:

https://www.amazon.com/author/faisal.jamil

Email: faisaljamilauthor@gmail.com

MASTERING TERRITORY MANAGEMENT STRATEGIES FOR SUCCESS

Introduction

Territory management is a crucial aspect of business that involves dividing geographical areas into manageable segments to maximize sales and customer satisfaction. This book provides a comprehensive guide to mastering territory management, offering strategies, tips, and best practices for success.

Table of Content

Preface	8
Chapter 1: Understanding Territory Management	9
Chapter 2: Analyzing Territory Potential	16
Chapter 3: Developing a Territory Plan	22
Chapter 4: Territory Mapping and Alignment	28
Chapter 5: Managing Customer Relationships	33
Chapter 6: Sales Forecasting and Performance Evaluation	38
Chapter 7: Territory Expansion and Growth	43
Chapter 8: Technology in Territory Management	48
Chapter 9: Managing Territory Teams	53
Chapter 10: Adapting to Changing Market Conditions	58
Conclusion	63

Preface

Welcome to "Mastering Territory Management: Strategies for Success." This book is designed to be a comprehensive guide for individuals and businesses looking to enhance their territory management skills and drive exceptional results. Territory management is a critical aspect of sales and marketing, as it involves dividing geographic regions to maximize sales and customer coverage.

Effective territory management can lead to optimized resource allocation, enhanced customer service, and increased sales revenue. However, mastering territory management requires a deep understanding of key concepts, principles, and strategies.

In this book, we will explore the definition and importance of territory management, as well as key concepts such as territory segmentation, sales forecasting, and customer relationship management. We will also provide practical guidance on analyzing territory potential, developing a territory plan, and managing customer relationships.

Each chapter is designed to be informative and actionable, providing you with the knowledge and tools you need to succeed in territory management. Whether you are a sales manager, business owner, or sales professional, this book is intended to be a valuable resource that will help you optimize your territory management practices and achieve sustainable growth and success.

We hope that you find this book to be informative and inspiring. Thank you for choosing "Mastering Territory Management: Strategies for Success."

Chapter 1

Understanding Territory Management

A: Definition of Territory Management:

Territory management is a strategic approach used by businesses to divide geographic regions into manageable segments in order to maximize sales and customer coverage. It involves a comprehensive analysis of market potential, the strategic assignment of resources such as sales representatives, and the implementation of tailored strategies to achieve specific business goals within each territory.

Key Components of Territory Management:

1: Market Analysis:

Territory management begins with a thorough analysis of the market within each geographic region. This includes understanding the demographics, buying behaviors, and preferences of customers in that area.

2: Resource Allocation:

Based on the market analysis, resources such as sales personnel, marketing budgets, and inventory are allocated to each territory. This ensures that the right resources are in place to effectively reach and serve customers.

3: Strategic Planning:

Once resources are allocated, a strategic plan is developed for each territory. This plan outlines the goals, objectives, and strategies that will be used to achieve success within that specific region.

4: Implementation:

With a strategic plan in place, the strategies are implemented within each territory. This may include activities such as sales promotions, advertising campaigns, and customer outreach efforts.

5: Monitoring and Adjustment:

Territory management is an ongoing process that requires constant monitoring and adjustment. By tracking key performance indicators (KPIs) and customer feedback, businesses can make informed decisions and adjust strategies as needed to ensure success within each territory.

Benefits of Territory Management:

1: Optimized Resource Allocation:

By dividing territories strategically, businesses can allocate resources more efficiently, maximizing their return on investment.

2: Enhanced Customer Service:

Territory management allows businesses to provide more personalized customer service by assigning dedicated sales representatives to each territory.

3: Increased Sales Revenue:

Effective territory management can lead to increased sales revenue by targeting high-potential markets and optimizing sales strategies within each territory.

4: Improved Market Coverage:

By dividing territories effectively, businesses can ensure that they are reaching all potential customers within their target market.

In conclusion, territory management is a strategic approach that allows businesses to maximize sales and customer coverage within geographic regions. By analyzing market potential, allocating resources strategically, and implementing tailored strategies, businesses can achieve their goals and drive success within each territory.

B: Importance of Effective Territory Management:

Effective territory management is crucial for business success for several reasons:

1: Optimized Resource Allocation:

By dividing territories based on factors such as demographics, purchasing behavior, and market potential, companies can allocate resources more efficiently. This leads to cost savings and increased profitability as resources are directed to where they are most needed and can yield the highest returns.

2: Maximized Sales Potential:

Territory management helps identify high-potential areas and allows companies to focus their sales and marketing efforts. By targeting specific territories with tailored strategies, companies can increase sales and market share. This targeted approach also helps in identifying and capitalizing on emerging market trends and opportunities.

3: Enhanced Customer Service:

Assigning dedicated sales representatives to specific territories enables companies to provide personalized service to customers. This leads to higher levels of customer satisfaction and loyalty, as customers feel valued and understood. Strong customer relationships built through effective territory management can result in repeat business and positive word-of-mouth referrals.

4: Improved Market Coverage:

Territory management enables companies to cover a broader market by strategically expanding into new territories. This expansion allows companies to reach new customers and increase their market share. By carefully planning and executing territory expansion, companies can tap into new markets and drive business growth.

5: Better Decision-Making:

By regularly analyzing territory performance and market trends, companies can make informed decisions about resource allocation, product positioning, and sales strategies. This data-driven approach allows companies to identify areas for improvement and adjust their strategies accordingly. It also helps in identifying and mitigating potential risks and challenges before they become major issues.

In conclusion, effective territory management is essential for business success as it allows companies to optimize resource allocation, maximize sales potential, enhance customer service, improve market coverage, and make better-informed decisions. By implementing effective territory management strategies, companies can achieve sustainable growth and maintain a competitive edge in the market.

C: Key Concepts and Principles:

1: Territory Segmentation:

Dividing territories based on factors such as geography, demographics, and market potential to optimize sales and resource allocation. By segmenting territories, businesses can tailor their sales and marketing strategies to specific customer segments, leading to increased efficiency and effectiveness in reaching target markets.

2: Sales Territory Design:

Designing territories with clearly defined boundaries, assigned sales representatives, and specific goals and objectives. Effective territory design ensures that each territory is manageable and that sales representatives have a clear understanding of their responsibilities and targets.

3: Territory Alignment:

Aligning territories with overall business objectives and sales strategies to ensure that each territory contributes effectively to the company's goals. Territory alignment involves ensuring that territories are balanced in terms of potential, workload, and resources, and that they are in line with the company's market expansion and growth objectives.

4: Territory Analysis:

Regularly analyzing territories to assess performance, identify opportunities for improvement, and make data-driven decisions. Territory analysis involves evaluating factors such as sales performance, customer demographics, market trends, and competitor activity to identify areas where adjustments can be made to improve sales and profitability.

5: Territory Planning:

Developing comprehensive plans for each territory, including setting sales targets, defining strategies, and allocating resources to achieve sales goals. Territory planning involves creating a roadmap for sales activities, outlining the steps needed to achieve targets, and ensuring that resources are allocated effectively to support sales efforts.

6: Territory Evaluation:

Evaluating the effectiveness of territory management strategies, measuring performance against targets, and identifying areas for adjustment and improvement. Territory evaluation involves reviewing sales data, customer feedback, and market trends to assess the impact of territory management strategies and identify areas where changes may be needed to improve performance.

In conclusion, understanding the definition, importance, and key concepts of territory management is essential for businesses to effectively manage their territories, optimize sales performance, and achieve sustainable growth. By implementing these principles, businesses can enhance their territory management practices and drive success in their sales operations.

Chapter 2
Analyzing Territory Potential

A: Methods for Assessing Territory Potential:

1: Market Research:

Conducting market research to gather data on customer demographics, purchasing behavior, and market trends to assess the potential of each territory. Market research helps businesses understand the size and characteristics of their target market, identify growth opportunities, and make informed decisions about resource allocation and strategy development.

2: Sales Data Analysis:

Analyzing past sales data to identify patterns, trends, and opportunities for growth within each territory. Sales data analysis helps businesses identify high-performing territories, understand factors driving sales performance, and identify areas for improvement.

3: Competitor Analysis:

Studying competitor activity and market share to understand the competitive landscape and assess the potential of each territory. Competitor analysis helps businesses identify competitive threats, benchmark their performance against competitors, and develop strategies to differentiate themselves in the market.

4: Customer Surveys:

Conducting surveys to gather feedback from customers within each territory to understand their needs, preferences, and buying behavior. Customer surveys help businesses gather insights directly from their target market, identify areas for improvement, and tailor their products and services to better meet customer needs.

5: Field Visits:

Sending sales representatives to visit territories to gather firsthand insights into market conditions, customer preferences, and competitor activity. Field visits allow businesses to gather real-time information, build relationships with customers, and identify opportunities for growth and improvement.

By utilizing these methods for assessing territory potential, businesses can gain a comprehensive understanding of their target market, identify growth opportunities, and develop strategies to maximize sales and profitability within each territory.

B: Factors Influencing Territory Potential:

1: Demographics:

Population size, age distribution, income levels, and other demographic factors can influence the potential of a territory. For example, a territory with a large population of young adults with high disposable income may have higher sales potential for certain products or services.

2: Market Size:

The size of the market in terms of the number of potential customers and their purchasing power can indicate the potential of a territory. A larger market size typically indicates greater sales potential, but other factors such as competition and market saturation should also be considered.

3: Competition:

The level of competition in a territory, including the number of competitors and their market share, can impact the potential of the territory. High competition can make it more challenging to gain market share, while low competition may present opportunities for growth.

4: Economic Conditions:

Economic factors such as GDP growth, employment rates, and consumer spending can affect the potential of a territory. Territories with strong economic growth and high consumer confidence may have greater sales potential than territories with weaker economic conditions.

5: Infrastructure:

The presence of infrastructure such as transportation networks, communication systems, and distribution channels can influence the potential of a territory. Good infrastructure can facilitate business operations and make it easier to reach customers, potentially increasing sales potential.

6: Regulatory Environment:

Regulatory factors such as government policies, trade regulations, and industry standards can impact the potential of a territory. A favorable regulatory environment can create opportunities for business growth, while unfavorable regulations may pose challenges.

By considering these factors when assessing territory potential, businesses can make informed decisions about resource allocation, strategy development, and market expansion, ultimately maximizing sales and profitability within each territory.

C: Tools and Techniques for Analysis:

1: GIS Mapping:

Geographic Information System (GIS) mapping software can be used to visualize and analyze territory boundaries, demographics, and market potential. GIS mapping allows businesses to identify patterns, trends, and opportunities within each territory, helping them make informed decisions about resource allocation and market expansion.

2: CRM Software:

Customer Relationship Management (CRM) software can track customer interactions, sales data, and market trends to provide insights into territory potential. CRM software allows businesses to analyze customer behavior, identify sales opportunities, and tailor their marketing strategies to specific territories.

3: Market Segmentation Analysis:

Using market segmentation techniques to divide the market into segments based on demographics, behavior, and other factors to assess territory potential. Market segmentation analysis helps businesses understand their target market better, identify customer needs, and develop targeted marketing strategies for each segment.

4: SWOT Analysis:

Conducting a SWOT (Strengths, Weaknesses, Opportunities, Threats) analysis to identify internal and external factors that can impact territory potential. SWOT analysis helps businesses assess their competitive position, identify areas for improvement, and develop strategies to capitalize on opportunities and mitigate threats.

5: Statistical Analysis:

Using statistical tools and techniques to analyze sales data, customer surveys, and other data sources to assess territory potential. Statistical analysis helps businesses identify trends, patterns, and correlations within their data, providing valuable insights into customer behavior and market dynamics.

By using these methods, analyzing these factors, and employing these tools and techniques, businesses can effectively assess the potential of their territories and make informed decisions to optimize resource allocation and maximize sales performance.

Chapter 3
Developing a Territory Plan

A: Steps to Creating a Territory Plan:

1: Define Territory Objectives:

Clearly define the objectives of the territory plan, such as increasing sales, expanding market share, or improving customer satisfaction. Objectives should be specific, measurable, achievable, relevant, and time-bound (SMART).

2: Conduct Territory Analysis:

Analyze the current state of the territory, including market potential, competition, and customer needs. This analysis provides the foundation for developing strategies and setting goals.

3: Set Territory Goals:

Based on the analysis, set specific, measurable, achievable, relevant, and time-bound (SMART) goals for the territory. Goals should align with the overall business objectives and address key areas for improvement.

4: Develop Strategies:

Develop strategies to achieve the goals, such as targeting specific customer segments, expanding product offerings, or improving sales processes. Strategies should be tailored to the unique characteristics of the territory and the needs of its customers.

5: Allocate Resources:

Determine the resources needed to implement the strategies, including sales personnel, marketing budget, and support services. Allocate resources based on the priorities identified in the territory analysis and the goals set for the territory.

6: Create Action Plan:

Develop a detailed action plan outlining the steps to be taken, timelines, responsibilities, and milestones. The action plan should provide a roadmap for implementing the strategies and achieving the goals of the territory plan.

7: Implement Plan:

Execute the action plan, monitor progress, and make adjustments as needed. Communication and coordination among team members are crucial during the implementation phase to ensure that the plan is executed effectively.

8: Evaluate Performance:

Regularly evaluate the performance of the territory plan against the set goals and objectives. Use key performance indicators (KPIs) to track progress and identify areas for improvement.

9: Review and Adjust:

Based on the evaluation, review the territory plan and make adjustments to improve performance and achieve the desired outcomes. Territory plans should be flexible and adaptive to changing market conditions and business priorities.

By following these steps, businesses can create effective territory plans that drive sales growth, improve customer satisfaction, and achieve sustainable business success.

B: Setting Goals and Objectives:

1: Sales Targets:

Set specific sales targets for the territory, taking into account past performance, market potential, and business objectives. Sales targets should be realistic and achievable, yet challenging enough to drive performance.

2: Market Share:

Determine the desired market share for the territory and develop strategies to achieve it. This could include targeting specific customer segments, expanding distribution channels, or launching marketing campaigns to increase brand awareness.

3: Customer Satisfaction:

Set goals for improving customer satisfaction, such as increasing repeat business or reducing customer complaints. This could involve improving customer service processes, enhancing product quality, or implementing loyalty programs.

4: Product Penetration:

Set goals for increasing the penetration of existing products or launching new products in the territory. This could involve identifying cross-selling or upselling opportunities, conducting market research to identify unmet needs, or developing new product offerings.

5: Revenue Growth:

Establish goals for revenue growth, taking into account factors such as pricing, product mix, and market demand. This could involve developing pricing strategies, introducing new revenue streams, or expanding into new market segments.

Setting clear and measurable goals and objectives is essential for guiding the territory plan and measuring its success. Goals should be aligned with overall business objectives and reflect the unique characteristics and opportunities of the territory. Regular monitoring and evaluation of progress towards these goals will help ensure that the territory plan remains on track and delivers the desired outcomes.

C: Strategies for Implementation:

1: Segmentation and Targeting:

Segment the market based on factors such as demographics, behavior, and needs, and target specific segments with tailored marketing messages and offers. This approach allows businesses to focus their resources on the most profitable customer segments and increase the effectiveness of their marketing efforts.

2: Product Positioning:

Position products or services in the territory to meet the needs and preferences of the target market and differentiate them from competitors. Effective product positioning helps businesses create a strong brand identity and attract customers who are willing to pay a premium for their products or services.

3: Sales Force Deployment:

Deploy sales personnel strategically to cover the territory effectively and maximize sales opportunities. This may involve assigning sales representatives based on their expertise, experience, and knowledge of the territory to ensure that they can effectively engage with customers and drive sales.

4: Marketing and Promotion:

Develop marketing campaigns and promotional activities to raise awareness and generate interest in the territory. This could include advertising, public relations, social media marketing, and other promotional efforts to attract customers and increase sales.

5: Customer Relationship Management:

Implement CRM systems and processes to manage customer relationships effectively and enhance customer loyalty. By keeping track of customer interactions and preferences, businesses can personalize their marketing efforts and provide better service to customers, leading to increased customer satisfaction and loyalty.

6: Training and Development:

Provide training and development opportunities for sales personnel to enhance their skills and knowledge, improving their performance in the territory. This could include sales training, product knowledge sessions, and professional development programs to help sales representatives better understand the market and serve customers effectively.

By following these steps, setting clear goals and objectives, and implementing effective strategies, businesses can develop a territory plan that maximizes sales and achieves sustainable growth in their target markets.

Chapter 4
Territory Mapping and Alignment

A: Techniques for Territory Mapping:

1: Geographic Information System (GIS):

GIS software can be used to create detailed maps that show geographical boundaries, customer locations, and other relevant data. GIS technology allows businesses to visualize and analyze spatial data, helping them make informed decisions about territory boundaries and resource allocation.

2: Data Analysis:

Analyzing demographic, sales, and customer data can help identify patterns and trends that can be used to create effective territory maps. By analyzing data, businesses can identify areas with high potential for sales growth and allocate resources accordingly.

3: Market Potential Analysis:

Assessing the market potential of different areas can help determine how territories should be divided to maximize sales opportunities. Market potential analysis involves evaluating factors such as population size, income levels, and competitor activity to identify areas with high growth potential.

4: Sales Data Mapping:

Mapping sales data can help identify areas with high and low sales performance, which can inform territory mapping decisions. By visualizing sales data on a map, businesses can identify patterns and trends that can help them optimize their territory boundaries.

5: Customer Segmentation:

Segmenting customers based on factors such as demographics, purchasing behavior, and location can help create territories that are tailored to specific customer needs. By understanding the unique needs of different customer segments, businesses can create territories that are more likely to result in sales success.

By utilizing these techniques for territory mapping, businesses can create well-defined territories that are optimized for sales success and customer satisfaction.

B: Aligning Territories with Company Objectives:

1: Sales Goals:

Aligning territories with company sales goals ensures that each territory contributes to the overall sales targets of the organization. By aligning territories with sales goals, businesses can ensure that resources are allocated effectively to maximize sales performance and achieve desired outcomes.

2: Market Coverage:

Ensuring that territories are aligned with market potential helps maximize sales opportunities and market penetration. By aligning territories with market potential, businesses can focus their efforts on areas with the highest potential for growth and profitability.

3: Customer Service:

Aligning territories with customer locations and needs helps provide better customer service and support. By aligning territories with customer locations, businesses can ensure that customers are served effectively and efficiently, leading to increased satisfaction and loyalty.

4: Resource Allocation:

Aligning territories with resource allocation ensures that sales resources such as personnel, budget, and marketing efforts are allocated effectively to achieve the desired results. By aligning territories with resource allocation, businesses can optimize their resources and maximize their return on investment.

5: Profitability:

Aligning territories with profitability targets helps ensure that resources are focused on high-profit areas, maximizing overall profitability for the company. By aligning territories with profitability targets, businesses can prioritize efforts in areas that are most likely to generate profits, leading to increased profitability and growth.

By aligning territories with company objectives, businesses can ensure that their territory management strategies are aligned with their overall business goals, leading to increased efficiency, effectiveness, and profitability.

C: Best Practices for Territory Alignment:

1: Regular Review:

Regularly review and update territory maps to ensure they remain aligned with company objectives and market conditions. Market dynamics can change rapidly, so it's important to regularly review territories to ensure they are optimized for current conditions.

2: Collaboration:

Involve sales teams, managers, and other stakeholders in the territory alignment process to ensure buy-in and effectiveness. By involving key stakeholders in the process, businesses can ensure that territories are aligned with their needs and objectives, leading to greater success.

3: Flexibility:

Be flexible and willing to adjust territory boundaries and assignments based on changing market conditions and business needs. Flexibility is key in territory alignment, as market conditions and business priorities can change rapidly. Being able to adapt quickly to these changes ensures that territories remain effective and efficient.

4: Data-Driven Decisions:

Use data and analytics to inform territory alignment decisions, ensuring they are based on objective criteria rather than subjective opinions. Data-driven decision-making helps businesses create territories that are based on empirical evidence, leading to more effective outcomes.

5: Communication:

Clearly communicate territory changes to all stakeholders to ensure everyone is aware of the new alignments and their implications. Effective communication is essential in territory alignment, as it ensures that everyone is on the same page and understands the rationale behind the changes.

By using these techniques, aligning territories with company objectives, and following best practices for territory alignment, businesses can create effective territory maps that maximize sales opportunities, improve customer service, and drive overall business success.

Chapter 5

Managing Customer Relationships

A: Building and Maintaining Customer Relationships:

1: Personalization:

Tailor interactions to meet the individual needs and preferences of each customer, building a more personalized relationship. By understanding each customer's unique needs and preferences, businesses can create a more meaningful and engaging experience that fosters loyalty and trust.

2: Regular Communication:

Keep in touch with customers through regular communication channels such as emails, phone calls, and newsletters to maintain engagement. Regular communication helps businesses stay top-of-mind with customers and allows them to provide updates, promotions, and valuable information that can enhance the customer experience.

3: Customer Feedback:

Actively seek feedback from customers to understand their needs and expectations, demonstrating a commitment to their satisfaction. Customer feedback is invaluable for businesses as it provides insights into areas for improvement and helps them better understand customer needs and preferences.

4: Value Addition:

Offer value-added services or products that enhance the customer experience and demonstrate a commitment to their success. By providing additional value beyond the core product or service, businesses can differentiate themselves from competitors and build stronger, more loyal customer relationships.

5: Customer Loyalty Programs:

Implement loyalty programs to reward repeat customers and incentivize them to continue doing business with you. Loyalty programs can help businesses retain customers, increase customer lifetime value, and create advocates who can help promote their brand to others.

6: Customer Service:

Provide excellent customer service, resolving issues promptly and efficiently to build trust and loyalty. Customer service is a key driver of customer satisfaction and loyalty. By providing exceptional customer service, businesses can create positive experiences that keep customers coming back.

By implementing these strategies, businesses can build and maintain strong customer relationships that drive loyalty, repeat business, and long-term success.

B: Strategies for Effective Communication:

1: Clear and Concise Messaging:

Ensure that communication is clear, concise, and easily understood to avoid misunderstandings. Use simple language and avoid jargon or technical terms that may confuse the audience.

2: Multichannel Communication:

Use multiple communication channels such as email, phone, and social media to reach customers and accommodate their preferences. By using multiple channels, businesses can reach a wider audience and ensure that their message is heard.

3: Two-Way Communication:

Encourage two-way communication by actively listening to customer feedback and responding promptly. Two-way communication allows businesses to engage with customers, address their concerns, and build stronger relationships.

4: Personalized Communication:

Personalize communication by addressing customers by name and tailoring messages to their specific needs and interests. Personalization helps businesses create more meaningful interactions with customers and increases the likelihood of engagement.

5: Consistent Communication:

Maintain consistent communication with customers to keep them engaged and informed about your products or services. Consistent communication helps build trust and loyalty with customers and keeps your brand top-of-mind.

By implementing these strategies, businesses can improve their communication with customers, build stronger relationships, and drive better business outcomes.

C: Handling Customer Complaints and Feedback:

1: Listen Actively:

Listen to customer complaints and feedback attentively, showing empathy and understanding. Let customers express their concerns fully before responding, and ensure they feel heard and understood.

2: Resolve Issues Quickly:

Resolve customer complaints and issues promptly, demonstrating a commitment to customer satisfaction. Take immediate action to address the problem and provide a satisfactory solution to the customer.

3: Apologize if Necessary:

If a mistake has been made, apologize sincerely and take steps to rectify the situation. Acknowledge the customer's inconvenience and offer a genuine apology to show that their experience is important to you.

4: Follow Up:

Follow up with customers after resolving their complaints to ensure their satisfaction and show that their feedback is valued. A follow-up call or email can help solidify the resolution and leave a positive impression on the customer.

5: Learn from Feedback:

Use customer feedback as an opportunity to improve products, services, and processes, demonstrating a commitment to continuous improvement. Analyze the feedback received and use it to make meaningful changes that address customer concerns and enhance their experience.

By implementing these strategies, businesses can effectively manage customer relationships, build loyalty, and drive long-term success. Handling customer complaints and feedback in a professional and proactive manner can turn a negative experience into a positive one, leading to increased customer satisfaction and loyalty.

Chapter 6

Sales Forecasting and Performance Evaluation

A: Importance of Sales Forecasting:

1: Planning and Budgeting:

Sales forecasting helps businesses plan and budget effectively by providing insight into expected sales revenues. It allows businesses to anticipate future sales trends and adjust their plans and budgets accordingly.

2: Resource Allocation:

It enables businesses to allocate resources such as sales personnel, marketing budget, and inventory more efficiently based on anticipated sales volumes. By aligning resources with expected sales, businesses can optimize their operations and maximize profitability.

3: Setting Realistic Goals:

Sales forecasting helps set realistic sales targets and goals, which can motivate sales teams and drive performance. By providing a clear target to work towards, sales forecasting can help focus efforts and improve sales outcomes.

4: Risk Management:

By identifying potential sales fluctuations, businesses can proactively manage risks and mitigate potential losses. Sales forecasting allows businesses to anticipate changes in demand and take steps to minimize the impact of unforeseen events.

5: Decision Making:

Sales forecasting provides valuable information for decision making, such as pricing strategies, product launches, and market expansion plans. By using sales forecasts as a basis for decision making, businesses can make informed choices that are more likely to lead to success.

In conclusion, sales forecasting is a valuable tool for businesses of all sizes, providing insight into future sales trends and helping to inform strategic decisions. By accurately forecasting sales, businesses can improve planning, allocate resources more effectively, and ultimately drive growth and profitability.

B: Methods for Forecasting Sales:

1: Historical Data Analysis:

Analyzing past sales data to identify trends and patterns that can be used to predict future sales. By examining historical sales data, businesses can identify seasonal trends, growth patterns, and other factors that can help forecast future sales.

2: Market Research:

Conducting market research to gather data on customer preferences, buying behavior, and market trends that can inform sales forecasts. Market research can provide valuable insights into customer needs and competitive dynamics, helping businesses make more accurate sales forecasts.

3: Regression Analysis:

Using statistical regression models to analyze the relationship between sales and various factors such as price, promotion, and seasonality. Regression analysis can help businesses quantify the impact of different variables on sales and make more accurate sales forecasts.

4: Qualitative Methods:

Gathering input from sales teams, industry experts, and customers to make informed judgments about future sales. Qualitative methods can provide valuable insights into market dynamics and customer preferences that may not be captured by quantitative data alone.

5: Time Series Analysis:

Using time series models to forecast sales based on historical data, taking into account trends, seasonality, and other factors. Time series analysis can help businesses predict future sales based on past patterns, making it a valuable tool for sales forecasting.

By using these methods in combination, businesses can develop more accurate sales forecasts that can help them make informed decisions and achieve their sales goals.

C: Evaluating Sales Performance in Territories:

1: Sales Targets vs. Actual Sales:

Comparing actual sales against targets set in the territory plan to assess performance. This comparison helps businesses understand whether they are on track to meet their sales goals and identify areas where performance may be falling short.

2: Market Share:

Monitoring market share to evaluate the effectiveness of sales strategies and tactics in capturing market share. By tracking market share, businesses can assess their competitive position and adjust their strategies to increase market share if necessary.

3: Customer Acquisition and Retention:

Tracking customer acquisition and retention rates to gauge the effectiveness of customer relationship management strategies. This metric helps businesses understand how well they are attracting and retaining customers, which is critical for long-term success.

4: Sales Conversion Rates:

Analyzing sales conversion rates to assess the effectiveness of sales efforts in converting leads into customers. By tracking conversion rates, businesses can identify opportunities to improve their sales processes and increase conversion rates.

5: Profitability:

Evaluating the profitability of sales in each territory to determine the return on investment and identify areas for improvement. By analyzing profitability, businesses can identify high-profit areas and allocate resources accordingly to maximize profitability.

By utilizing these methods for forecasting sales and evaluating sales performance in territories, businesses can make informed decisions, optimize sales strategies, and drive sustainable growth. Evaluating sales performance helps businesses identify strengths and weaknesses in their sales efforts and make adjustments to improve performance and achieve their sales goals.

Chapter 7
Territory Expansion and Growth

A: Identifying Opportunities for Expansion:

1: Market Research:

Conducting market research to identify new geographical areas or customer segments with growth potential. Market research helps businesses understand market dynamics, customer needs, and competitive landscape, providing insights into where expansion opportunities may lie.

2: Competitor Analysis:

Analyzing competitor activity to identify gaps in the market and opportunities for expansion. By studying competitors, businesses can identify areas where they can differentiate themselves and gain a competitive advantage in new markets.

3: Customer Feedback:

Gathering feedback from existing customers to understand their needs and identify areas for expansion. Customer feedback can provide valuable insights into new products or services that may appeal to existing customers or new customer segments.

4: Industry Trends:

Monitoring industry trends and developments to identify emerging markets or products with growth potential. By staying abreast of industry trends, businesses can identify new opportunities for expansion and position themselves to capitalize on emerging market trends.

5: Partnerships and Alliances:

Forming partnerships or alliances with other businesses to access new markets or distribution channels. Collaborating with other businesses can help businesses expand into new markets more quickly and cost-effectively by leveraging existing networks and resources.

By utilizing these methods for identifying opportunities for expansion, businesses can identify new markets, products, or customer segments with growth potential, enabling them to expand their operations and drive business growth. Identifying opportunities for expansion is essential for businesses looking to grow and stay competitive in today's dynamic marketplace.

B: Strategies for Growing Territories:

1: Market Penetration:

Increasing market share in existing territories by targeting new customers or expanding product offerings. This strategy focuses on maximizing sales from existing customers and markets.

2: Market Development:

Expanding into new geographical areas or customer segments with tailored marketing strategies. This strategy involves identifying and entering new markets to increase sales and diversify revenue streams.

3: Product Development:

Introducing new products or services to existing territories to stimulate growth and attract new customers. This strategy involves innovating and expanding product lines to meet evolving customer needs and preferences.

4: Diversification:

Diversifying product offerings or entering new markets to reduce risk and capitalize on new opportunities. This strategy involves expanding into unrelated markets or industries to create new revenue streams and reduce dependence on existing markets.

5: Acquisitions and Mergers:

Acquiring or merging with other businesses to expand market reach and customer base. This strategy involves purchasing or combining with other companies to gain access to new markets, technologies, or resources.

By utilizing these strategies for growing territories, businesses can expand their operations, increase market share, and drive sustainable growth. Implementing these strategies requires careful planning, market analysis, and execution to ensure success and maximize returns.

C: Overcoming Challenges in Territory Expansion:

1: Resource Constraints:

Limited resources such as budget, manpower, and infrastructure can hinder expansion efforts. Solutions include prioritizing resources, seeking external funding, or outsourcing certain functions to maximize efficiency and effectiveness.

2: Competition:

Intense competition in new markets can make it challenging to gain market share. Strategies to overcome this challenge include differentiation, pricing strategies, and customer relationship management to create a unique value proposition for customers.

3: Regulatory Issues:

Compliance with regulations in new territories can be complex. Solutions include thorough research, legal consultation, and implementation of compliance management systems to ensure adherence to local laws and regulations.

4: Cultural Differences:

Adapting to cultural differences in new markets requires cultural sensitivity and tailored marketing strategies. Businesses should invest in understanding local customs, traditions, and preferences to effectively engage with the target audience.

5: Logistical Challenges:

Managing logistics such as distribution, inventory, and supply chain in new territories requires efficient planning and execution. Businesses should invest in robust logistics management systems and partnerships to ensure smooth operations.

By identifying opportunities for expansion, implementing growth strategies, and effectively overcoming these challenges, businesses can successfully expand their territories and achieve sustainable growth in new markets.

Chapter 8

Technology in Territory Management

A: Role of Technology in Territory Management:

1: Data Analysis:

Technology enables businesses to analyze large amounts of data to identify trends, patterns, and opportunities in territories. By leveraging data analytics tools, businesses can make informed decisions and optimize their territory management strategies.

2: Communication:

Technology facilitates communication between sales teams, managers, and customers, enabling real-time collaboration and feedback. Communication tools such as email, messaging apps, and video conferencing platforms help streamline communication and improve coordination within the sales team.

3: Automation:

Technology automates repetitive tasks such as data entry, reporting, and scheduling, freeing up time for sales teams to focus on selling. Automation tools can improve efficiency, reduce errors, and enhance productivity in territory management.

4: Customer Relationship Management (CRM):

CRM systems help businesses manage customer relationships, track interactions, and personalize communication, improving customer engagement and loyalty. By centralizing customer data and interactions, CRM systems enable businesses to provide better service and support to their customers.

5: Mapping and Visualization:

Geographic Information System (GIS) technology allows businesses to map territories, visualize data, and identify areas for growth or optimization. By using GIS tools, businesses can optimize territory boundaries, target specific geographic areas, and analyze market potential more effectively.

Overall, technology plays a crucial role in territory management by enabling businesses to analyze data, communicate effectively, automate tasks, manage customer relationships, and visualize territories. By leveraging technology effectively, businesses can improve their territory management strategies and drive growth and profitability.

B: Tools and Software for Effective Territory Management:

1: CRM Software:

Customer Relationship Management (CRM) software such as Salesforce, HubSpot, and Zoho CRM helps businesses manage customer relationships, track sales, and analyze data. CRM software allows businesses to centralize customer information, track interactions, and improve communication with customers.

2: GIS Software:

Geographic Information System (GIS) software such as ArcGIS and Google Maps enables businesses to map territories, visualize data, and analyze geographic information. GIS software helps businesses understand their territories better, identify areas for growth, and optimize territory boundaries.

3: Sales Force Automation (SFA):

Sales Force Automation (SFA) software automates sales tasks such as lead management, opportunity tracking, and forecasting, improving sales efficiency. SFA software helps businesses streamline sales processes, reduce manual work, and improve sales productivity.

4: Business Intelligence (BI) Tools:

Business Intelligence (BI) tools such as Tableau and Power BI help businesses analyze data, generate insights, and make informed decisions. BI tools enable businesses to visualize sales data, identify trends, and optimize territory management strategies.

5: Mobile Applications:

Mobile apps enable sales teams to access customer information, update records, and communicate with customers and colleagues on the go, improving productivity and responsiveness. Mobile apps for territory management allow sales teams to stay connected and access important information from anywhere, helping them work more efficiently.

By utilizing these tools and software for effective territory management, businesses can improve their sales processes, optimize territory performance, and drive growth and profitability.

C: Integrating Technology into Territory Planning and Execution:

1: Data Integration:

Integrating data from various sources such as CRM systems, sales reports, and market research into a single platform for comprehensive analysis and decision-making. By integrating data, businesses can gain a holistic view of their territories and make informed decisions to optimize performance.

2: Workflow Automation:

Automating workflows such as lead routing, quote generation, and order processing to streamline operations and improve efficiency. Workflow automation helps businesses reduce manual tasks, minimize errors, and accelerate sales processes.

3: Real-Time Tracking:

Using GPS and mobile technology to track sales team activities, monitor performance, and optimize routes for better territory coverage. Real-time tracking enables businesses to respond quickly to changing market conditions and customer needs, improving overall sales effectiveness.

4: Predictive Analytics:

Utilizing predictive analytics to forecast sales, identify trends, and anticipate customer needs, enabling proactive decision-making. Predictive analytics helps businesses identify opportunities and risks in their territories, allowing them to adjust their strategies accordingly.

5: Training and Support:

Providing training and support to sales teams on using technology effectively to enhance their productivity and performance in territory management. Proper training ensures that sales teams are equipped with the skills and knowledge to leverage technology for optimal results.

By leveraging technology in territory management, businesses can improve efficiency, optimize resources, and drive growth in their territories. Integrating technology into territory planning and execution allows businesses to stay competitive in today's dynamic marketplace and achieve their sales objectives effectively.

Chapter 9

Managing Territory Teams

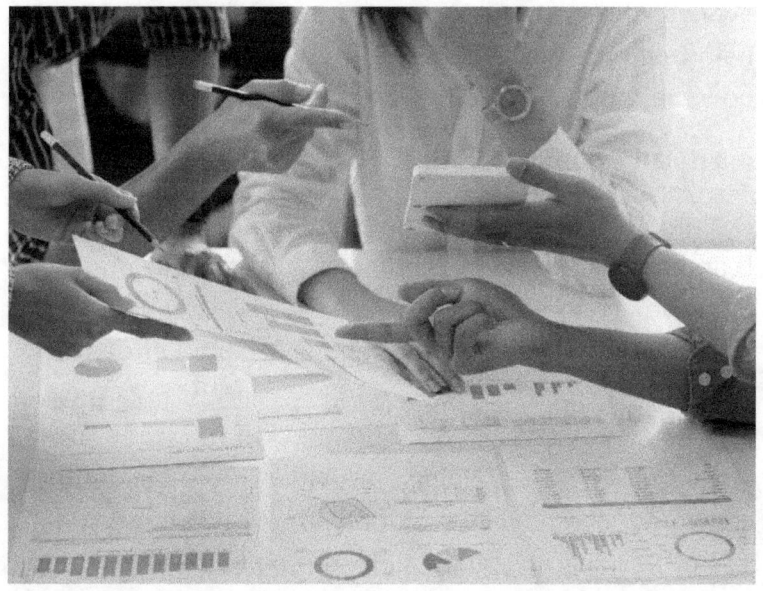

A: Building and Leading Successful Territory Teams:

1: Recruitment and Selection:

Recruit team members with the right skills, experience, and cultural fit for the territory team. Effective recruitment ensures that the team is composed of individuals who can contribute to its success.

2: Training and Development:

Provide ongoing training and development opportunities to enhance team members' skills and knowledge. Training ensures that team members are equipped to perform their roles effectively and adapt to changes in the market.

3: Clear Roles and Responsibilities:

Clearly define roles and responsibilities within the team to avoid confusion and improve efficiency. Clear expectations help team members understand their responsibilities and how they contribute to the overall goals of the team.

4: Effective Communication:

Foster open and transparent communication within the team to ensure that everyone is aligned and informed. Effective communication helps team members share information, resolve conflicts, and collaborate effectively.

5: Team Building Activities:

Organize team building activities to build trust, camaraderie, and collaboration among team members. Team building activities help strengthen relationships, improve morale, and create a positive team culture.

6: Performance Management:

Implement performance management systems to set goals, provide feedback, and reward high performance. Performance management helps track progress, identify areas for improvement, and recognize and reward team members' contributions.

By implementing these strategies, leaders can build and lead successful territory teams that are motivated, engaged, and effective in achieving their goals.

B: Motivating and Incentivizing Team Members:

1: Recognition and Rewards:

Recognize and reward team members for their achievements and contributions to motivate them. Recognition can be in the form of verbal praise, awards, or other tangible rewards to show appreciation for their efforts.

2: Career Growth Opportunities:

Provide opportunities for career growth and advancement to motivate team members to perform at their best. Career growth opportunities can include promotions, additional responsibilities, or training programs that help team members develop their skills and advance in their careers.

3: Incentive Programs:

Implement incentive programs such as bonuses, commissions, or awards to incentivize team members to achieve targets. Incentive programs provide a tangible reward for achieving specific goals and can help motivate team members to perform at a higher level.

4: Feedback and Coaching:

Provide regular feedback and coaching to help team members improve their performance and stay motivated. Feedback should be constructive, specific, and timely, and coaching should focus on developing skills and addressing any performance issues.

5: Work-Life Balance:

Promote work-life balance by offering flexible work arrangements and support for personal well-being. A healthy work-life balance is essential for maintaining motivation and preventing burnout among team members.

By implementing these strategies, leaders can motivate and incentivize team members to perform at their best, leading to improved morale, productivity, and performance within the territory team.

C: Resolving Conflicts within Territory Teams:

1: Identify the Root Cause:

Identify the underlying cause of the conflict and address it directly. Understanding the root cause of the conflict is essential for finding a lasting solution.

2: Open Communication:

Encourage open and honest communication among team members to resolve conflicts effectively. Create a safe space for team members to express their concerns and listen actively to each other's perspectives.

3: Mediation:

If necessary, involve a mediator or third party to help facilitate resolution. A mediator can help facilitate communication, clarify misunderstandings, and guide the parties toward a resolution.

4: Conflict Resolution Strategies:

Use conflict resolution strategies such as compromise, collaboration, or accommodation to find a mutually acceptable solution. Encourage team members to work together to find a solution that meets everyone's needs.

5: Follow-Up:

Follow up with team members after conflict resolution to ensure that the issue has been resolved satisfactorily and that there are no lingering tensions. Monitoring the situation after resolution can help prevent future conflicts and maintain a positive team dynamic.

By effectively resolving conflicts within territory teams, managers can create a positive work environment that fosters collaboration, productivity, and team cohesion.

Chapter 10

Adapting to Changing Market Conditions

A: Strategies for Adapting to Market Changes:

1: Market Research:

Conduct regular market research to stay informed about changing customer needs, preferences, and trends. Market research helps businesses anticipate market changes and adjust their strategies accordingly.

2: Agile Planning:

Adopt agile planning processes that allow for quick adjustments to strategies and tactics based on market changes. Agile planning enables businesses to respond rapidly to market shifts and stay ahead of the competition.

3: Diversification:

Diversify product offerings or target markets to reduce the impact of market fluctuations. Diversification spreads risk and allows businesses to capitalize on new opportunities that may arise in different market segments.

4: Customer Feedback:

Listen to customer feedback and use it to adapt products, services, and marketing strategies. Customer feedback provides valuable insights into customer needs and preferences, helping businesses tailor their offerings to meet customer expectations.

5: Competitor Analysis:

Monitor competitor activity and adjust strategies to maintain a competitive edge. Competitor analysis helps businesses identify emerging trends and threats in the market, enabling them to adjust their strategies accordingly.

6: Flexibility:

Maintain flexibility in operations, processes, and strategies to quickly respond to market changes. Flexibility allows businesses to adapt to changing market conditions and seize new opportunities as they arise.

By implementing these strategies, businesses can effectively adapt to market changes, stay competitive, and continue to grow and succeed in dynamic markets.

B: Forecasting and Planning for Market Fluctuations:

1: Scenario Planning:

Develop scenarios for different market conditions and plan responses accordingly. Scenario planning helps businesses prepare for various possibilities and react effectively to changes in the market.

2: Risk Management:

Identify potential risks and develop mitigation strategies to minimize their impact on operations. Risk management involves identifying, assessing, and prioritizing risks, and implementing measures to mitigate or control them.

3: Financial Planning:

Maintain a strong financial position and have contingency plans in place to weather market downturns. Financial planning involves forecasting financial outcomes, allocating resources effectively, and ensuring sufficient liquidity to meet obligations.

4: Collaboration:

Collaborate with suppliers, partners, and other stakeholders to share information and resources in response to market changes. Collaboration can help businesses leverage the strengths of their partners and respond more effectively to market fluctuations.

5: Continuous Monitoring:

Continuously monitor market conditions and performance indicators to identify trends and anticipate changes. By staying informed about market dynamics, businesses can adjust their strategies proactively and stay ahead of the competition.

By implementing these strategies, businesses can improve their ability to forecast and plan for market fluctuations, mitigate risks, and seize opportunities that arise in dynamic market environments.

C: Case Studies and Examples of Successful Adaptation:

1: Netflix:

Netflix successfully adapted to changing market conditions by transitioning from a DVD rental service to a streaming platform, responding to the shift in consumer preferences for online streaming. This shift allowed Netflix to expand its customer base globally and become a dominant player in the streaming industry.

2: Apple:

Apple continuously adapts its product offerings and marketing strategies to stay ahead of competitors and meet changing customer needs. For example, Apple regularly introduces new iPhone models with updated features and designs, as well as services like Apple Music to cater to the growing demand for digital content.

3: Amazon:

Amazon has adapted to changing market conditions by diversifying its product offerings, expanding into new markets, and investing in technology to improve customer experience and operational efficiency. Amazon's focus on innovation and customer-centric approach has helped it maintain its position as a leader in e-commerce and cloud computing.

4: Tesla:

Tesla has adapted to changing market conditions by focusing on electric vehicles and renewable energy products, responding to growing consumer demand for sustainable and eco-friendly alternatives. Tesla's innovative approach to product development and commitment to sustainability has helped it become a leader in the electric vehicle industry.

5: McDonald's:

McDonald's has adapted its menu and marketing strategies to cater to changing consumer preferences for healthier options. For example, McDonald's has introduced items such as salads and wraps alongside its traditional offerings to appeal to health-conscious consumers. This strategy has helped McDonald's maintain its relevance and appeal to a broader customer base.

By learning from these successful case studies, businesses can gain insights into effective adaptation strategies and apply them to their own operations. By forecasting and planning for market fluctuations, businesses can proactively respond to changes in the market and position themselves for long-term success.

Conclusion

Mastering territory management is crucial for businesses aiming to achieve sustainable growth and success. Effective territory management involves strategic planning, efficient resource allocation, and continuous performance evaluation to maximize sales and customer satisfaction. By implementing the strategies and practices outlined in this book, businesses can enhance their territory management skills and drive exceptional results.

Key strategies include:

1: Territory Segmentation:

Dividing territories based on factors like demographics, market potential, and customer behavior to optimize resource allocation and sales efforts.

2: Sales Forecasting:

Predicting future sales trends to make informed decisions and plan resources effectively.

3: Customer Relationship Management:

Building and maintaining strong customer relationships to enhance loyalty and drive sales growth.

4: Adapting to Market Changes:

Being agile and flexible to respond to changing market conditions and customer needs.

5: Team Management:

Building and leading successful territory teams through effective communication, motivation, and conflict resolution.

By mastering these strategies and practices, businesses can improve their territory management effectiveness, drive sales growth, and achieve sustainable business success.

www.ingramcontent.com/pod-product-compliance
Lightning Source LLC
Chambersburg PA
CBHW070413230526
45471CB00006B/2792